NICHOLAS WRIGHT

Nicholas Wright trained as an actor and joined the Royal Court Theatre in London as Casting Director before becoming the first Director of the Royal Court's Theatre Upstairs, where he presented an influential programme of new and first-time writing. From 1975 to 1977 he was joint Artistic Director of the Royal Court. He joined the National Theatre in 1984 as Literary Manager and was an Associate Director of the National until 1998.

His plays include *Treetops* and *One Fine Day* (Riverside Studios), *The Custom of the Country* and *The Desert Air* (RSC), *Cressida* (Almeida Theatre at the Albery), *Rattigan's Nijinsky* (Chichester), *The Last of the Duchess* (Hampstead Theatre) and *Mrs. Klein*, *Vincent in Brixton*, *The Reporter* and *Travelling Light* at the National Theatre. He adapted Philip Pullman's *His Dark Materials* for the National, where his versions of *John Gabriel Borkman* and *Three Sisters* were also produced. Other versions include *Naked* and *Lulu* for the Almeida and *Thérèse Raquin* for Chichester Festival Theatre. His adaptation of Pumla Gobodo-Madikizelas's *A Human Being Died That Night* was produced at Hampstead Theatre in 2013, his adaptation of Pat Barker's *Regeneration* was produced in Northampton and on tour in 2014, and his adaptation of Patrick Hamilton's *The Slaves of Solitude* was produced at Hampstead in 2017. His opera libretti are *The Little Prince* (composer Rachel Portman) for Houston Grand Opera, *Man on the Moon* (Jonathan Dove) for Channel 4 television and *Marnie* (Nico Muhly) for ENO in 2017 and the Met in 2018. Books are *99 Plays*, a survey of drama from Aeschylus until the present day, and *Changing Stages,* co-written with Richard Eyre.

Other Titles from Nick Hern Books

Annie Baker
THE FLICK
JOHN

Mike Bartlett
ALBION
BULL
GAME
AN INTERVENTION
KING CHARLES III
SNOWFLAKE
WILD

Howard Brenton
55 DAYS
#AIWW: THE ARREST OF AI WEIWEI
ANNE BOLEYN
BERLIN BERTIE
THE BLINDING LIGHT
DANCES OF DEATH *after* Strindberg
DOCTOR SCROGGY'S WAR
DRAWING THE LINE
ETERNAL LOVE
FAUST – PARTS ONE & TWO
    after Goethe
JUDE
LAWRENCE AFTER ARABIA
MISS JULIE & CREDITORS
    after Strindberg
NEVER SO GOOD
PAUL
THE RAGGED TROUSERED
    PHILANTHROPISTS *after* Tressell
THE SHADOW FACTORY Jez Butterworth
THE FERRYMAN
JERUSALEM
JEZ BUTTERWORTH PLAYS: ONE
JEZ BUTTERWORTH PLAYS: TWO
MOJO
THE NIGHT HERON
PARLOUR SONG
THE RIVER
THE WINTERLING

Caryl Churchill
BLUE HEART
CHURCHILL PLAYS: THREE
CHURCHILL PLAYS: FOUR
CHURCHILL PLAYS: FIVE
CHURCHILL: SHORTS
CLOUD NINE
DING DONG THE WICKED
A DREAM PLAY
    after Strindberg
DRUNK ENOUGH TO SAY I LOVE YOU?
ESCAPED ALONE
FAR AWAY
HERE WE GO
HOTEL
ICECREAM
LIGHT SHINING IN
    BUCKINGHAMSHIRE
LOVE AND INFORMATION
MAD FOREST
A NUMBER
PIGS AND DOGS
SEVEN JEWISH CHILDREN
THE SKRIKER
THIS IS A CHAIR
THYESTES *after* Seneca
TRAPS

Kevin Elyot
THE DAY I STOOD STILL
FORTY WINKS
KEVIN ELYOT: FOUR PLAYS
MOUTH TO MOUTH
MY NIGHT WITH REG

debbie tucker green
BORN BAD
DEBBIE TUCKER GREEN PLAYS: ONE
DIRTY BUTTERFLY
EAR FOR EYE
HANG
NUT
A PROFOUNDLY AFFECTIONATE,
PASSIONATE DEVOTION TO
    SOMEONE (– *NOUN*)
RANDOM
STONING MARY
TRADE & GENERATIONS
TRUTH AND RECONCILIATION

David Haig
THE GOOD SAMARITAN
MY BOY JACK
PRESSURE

Liz Lochhead
BLOOD AND ICE
DRACULA *after* Stoker
EDUCATING AGNES ('The School
    for Wives') *after* Molière
GOOD THINGS
LIZ LOCHHEAD: FIVE PLAYS
MARY QUEEN OF SCOTS GOT
    HER HEAD CHOPPED OFF
MEDEA *after* Euripides
MISERYGUTS & TARTUFFE
    after Molière
PERFECT DAYS
THEBANS
THON MAN MOLIÈRE

Conor McPherson
DUBLIN CAROL
GIRL FROM THE NORTH COUNTRY
    with Bob Dylan
McPHERSON PLAYS: ONE
McPHERSON PLAYS: TWO
McPHERSON PLAYS: THREE
THE NIGHT ALIVE
PORT AUTHORITY
THE SEAFARER
SHINING CITY
THE VEIL
THE WEIR

Nicholas Wright
CRESSIDA
HIS DARK MATERIALS *after* Pullman
THE LAST OF THE DUCHESS
LULU *after* Wedekind
MRS KLEIN
RATTIGAN'S NIJINSKY
REGENERATION *after* Pat Barker
THE REPORTER
THE SLAVES OF SOLITUDE
    after Patrick Hamilton
THÉRÈSE RAQUIN *after* Zola
THREE SISTERS *after* Chekhov
TRAVELLING LIGHT
VINCENT IN BRIXTON
WRIGHT: FIVE PLAYS

Nicholas Wright

8 HOTELS

NICK HERN BOOKS
London
www.nickhernbooks.co.uk

A Nick Hern Book

8 Hotels first published in Great Britain in 2019 as a paperback original by Nick Hern Books Limited, The Glasshouse, 49a Goldhawk Road, London W12 8QP

8 Hotels © 2019 Somerset West Limited
Introduction © 2019 Somerset West Limited

Nicholas Wright has asserted his right to be identified as the author of this work

'Ol' Man River' from *Show Boat,* lyrics by Oscar Hammerstein II. Every effort has been made to contact the copyright holders and obtain permission to reproduce this material.

Cover photograph: Paul Robeson (centre) and Jose Ferrer (right), watching softball with other members of the *Othello* cast, Central Park, New York City, circa 1943–44 (Everett Collection Inc./Alamy Stock Photo). Image design © Bob King Creative for Chichester Festival Theatre

Designed and typeset by Nick Hern Books, London
Printed and bound in Great Britain by Mimeo Ltd, Huntingdon, Cambridgeshire PE29 6XX

A CIP catalogue record for this book is available from the British Library

ISBN 978 1 84842 855 3

Introduction
Nicholas Wright

'I am so happy! I am *so happy!*' Uta clasped her arms around
herself, delightedly curled up in her chair, almost knocking her
head on the tablecloth. It was 1996, the start of the tour of my
play *Mrs Klein*, in which she was playing the title role. She, the
director William Carden and I were having dinner after the
show in an old, once-grand, now slightly dusty hotel in San
Francisco. Was she happy, I wondered, because the show had
gone well that night? Yes, very likely. And she liked long runs,
and she loved touring. But it felt as though something deeper
was in the air. It was she who had chosen this hotel: she had
made rather a point of it. Was this, I wondered, where she had
stayed over fifty years before on that wartime coast-to-coast
tour of *Othello* in which she played Desdemona, her husband
José Ferrer played Iago and Paul Robeson was the Moor? And
what did it mean to her to be there again?

That night is where my memory leads me, when I ask myself
the origin of this play.

I had never been so flattered in my life as when, a year or so
before that, William Carden – whom I didn't know – called me
from New York to say that Uta Hagen wanted to do my play.
Would I agree to that, he asked? I replied that I had idolised
Hagen ever since I'd seen her playing Martha in *Who's Afraid of
Virginia Woolf?* at the Piccadilly Theatre in 1963 and that, as far
as I was concerned, she could do whatever she wanted. She had
created the part on Broadway – it was her 'signature role', as
people say – and she was unforgettable in it: furious, funny,
heartfelt, wounded, unforgiving.

We all look different as we get older, but I think Uta changed
more than most of us. Photographs of her in that wartime
Othello show a blonde with the all-American cute good looks of

Rosemary Clooney. (Whom, oddly, José Ferrer would later marry not once but twice.) My memory of her in *Virginia Woolf* was of a rangy intellectual broad, almost mannish. When I finally met her in New York, in her little studio theatre where my play was being tried out, she was seventy-seven: gaunt and aquiline – 'eagle-like' – with burning energy and a warm voice that decades of smoking had touched with gravel. From time to time one caught a hint of a German accent: 'ex-OWS-sted', for 'exhausted'. Or was that the character taking over? She was still a magnificent actress and she was feisty. 'Oh, Uta,' said one of the other actresses, rather nervously, 'I'm leaving a little pause there. I hope it's okay with you?' Uta replied with spirit. 'Sure, sweetie, you leave that pause and I'll walk right off the stage because there won't be a damn thing to keep me on it.'

Robeson had first played Othello in 1930, in London during his and his wife's long, long stay in Britain. It was a fertile time for him: he starred onstage in *Show Boat*, he made some great recordings and some mediocre films, he became celebrated for his charm and looks, he was taken up by high society and he earned a fabulous amount of money. Britain was important to him for another reason: it was where his political awakening took place. He made an alliance with the struggling Welsh miners, whose love of song struck a chord in his heart. And through meeting African exiles like the future Ghanaian leader Kwame Nkrumah and the future Kenyan President Jomo Kenyatta… and also the great Trinidadian writer and thinker C. L. R. James… he discovered the anti-colonial cause that he would support for the rest of his life. By the time he returned to the USA, at the outbreak of World War II, he thought of himself as an activist first and an artist second. From now on, his acting and his singing, however highly he valued them, would be adjuncts to his political life: 'They give me a platform,' he would say.

For him to play Othello in the USA was a political message in itself. In 1940s America, actors of colour seldom appeared onstage except as servants, slaves and nannies. This was Robeson's chance to show a black man as a hero: brave, articulate and admired by all. He chose his director with care: Margaret Webster, an Englishwoman who was making a name

for herself in the USA as a Shakespeare specialist. She found
that casting would be tricky. For the part of Iago, she turned to
her friend Maurice Evans, a suavely decorous English actor
who was collaring the market in Shakespeare roles on
Broadway, but he turned her down. 'America isn't ready for
a black Othello,' he told her. Other offers produced the same
reply. It wasn't just fear of precedent: there was real alarm at the
prospect of a man of colour appearing in a romantic situation
with a white woman. (The African-American Ira Aldridge, a
celebrated Othello of the nineteenth century, played the role
throughout the length and breadth of Europe but never in his
home country.)

Just when it looked as though Iago would never be found,
Webster's partner – the actress Eva Le Gallienne – suggested
a young actor who had scored a hit in the vintage farce,
Charley's Aunt: his feat of diving horizontally into a Victorian
women's gown and emerging from the other end fully dressed
was a nightly showstopper. Once Ferrer was cast, it was only
natural for Desdemona to be offered to his young wife, Uta
Hagen. Webster had seen her, aged seventeen, as a sensational
Ophelia to Le Gallienne's Hamlet, and they'd recently played
together in *The Seagull* – Webster as Masha, Hagen as Nina – in
a revival starring America's theatrical royal couple, the Lunts.

Othello enjoyed a long Broadway run and then set out on a
nationwide tour. Now its political aim came into focus. It couldn't
tour to the American South: that would be crazy and unsafe. But
wherever it travelled, there would be theatres that had never
before hosted a racially integrated audience. Robeson, Webster
and the management insisted that performances should be open to
all, irrespective of colour or race, and the show held fast to this,
despite the occasional date where they found that white
ticketholders and those of colour had been deliberately seated on
opposite sides of the stalls with a kind of firebreak running down
the middle. There were other problems too. It wasn't unusual,
when Hagen, Ferrer and Robeson ate together in a restaurant, for
waiters to come rushing up to place discreet screens around them.
Some hotels operated a colour-bar, and there were times when
Robeson was asked politely if he would mind travelling in the

goods elevator in order not to upset the other guests, never mind that he was one of the most famous Americans in the world.

He would play Othello once again, in 1959 for the Shakespeare Memorial Theatre, as the RSC was then called. His passport had been taken away years before by the US State Department and there was no guarantee that he would get it back, so a standby actor was engaged, but Robeson arrived in Stratford-upon-Avon in time to rehearse and play. I was a drama student then, watching the show from the back of the stalls. It was thrilling to see this mighty character in the flesh. Some of his earlier magic was apparent, but not very much of it: one had to make allowances for his age. It was not long after this that he suffered a rapid deterioration in his health, the cause of which remains mysterious.

Margaret Webster's career in America never recovered from the setback that appears in the play. She returned to Britain, where she was thought reliable but old-fashioned and where she failed to find the prestigious work that she was used to. As a young actor, I auditioned for her in the Hampstead living room of her partner, the novelist Pamela Frankau. Frankau had written the play, which was modestly scheduled for a single week in Windsor. When one is an out-of-work actor, one places a lot of importance on the courtesy one is shown at auditions and, in this department, Webster received top marks from me: she was respectful of my terrible acting and turned me down with charm. I liked her a lot.

José Ferrer went on to enjoy a flourishing set of careers as actor, producer, director of plays and movie director. It was a matter of pride to him that in 1950, he became the first Latino to win an Academy Award for Best Actor: this was for *Cyrano de Bergerac*, which was also an iconic role of his on stage.

Uta continued acting for as long as the years allowed and became an important teacher. Her book, *Respect for Acting*, remains an essential guide for actors of today and of the future.

8 Hotels was first performed in the Minerva Theatre, Chichester, on 1 August 2019. The cast was as follows:

UTA HAGEN   Emma Paetz
JOSÉ FERRER (JOE)   Ben Cura
MARGARET WEBSTER (PEGGY)   Pandora Colin
PAUL ROBESON   Tory Kittles

Director   Richard Eyre
Designer   Rob Howell
Lighting Designer   Peter Mumford
Sound Designer   John Leonard
Video Designer   Andrzej Goulding
Casting Director   Charlotte Sutton CDG
US Casting   Jim Carnahan CSA

Company Dialect Work   Penny Dyer
Costume Supervisor   Lucy Gaiger
Props Supervisor   Sharon Foley
Hair, Wigs and Make-up   Campbell Young
                                             Associates
Assistant Director   Eva Sampson

Production Manager   Kate West
Company Stage Manager   Suzanne Bourke
Deputy Stage Manager   Lorna Earl
Assistant Stage Manager   Harriet Saffin

Characters

UTA HAGEN, *twenty-five*
JOSÉ FERRER (JOE), *thirty-two*
MARGARET WEBSTER (PEGGY), *thirty-nine*
PAUL ROBESON, *forty-six*

Time: 1944 and later

Place: The United States

The characters are American except for Peggy, who is English.
Their ages are given as at the start of the play.

*This text went to press before the end of rehearsals and so may
differ slightly from the play as performed.*

UTA

UTA. My first impression of Paul was that he took up half the
room. I mean the *personality* of him. His eyes were alive, his
confidence bounced off the walls and his smile was bright
enough to light a fire. He was also incredibly smart. I thought,
'He ought to be a politician.' Later, when I saw him speaking
at a rally, I realised that he already was one.

It started like this: Peggy had brought Joe and me for Paul to
look us over for her production of *Othello*: Joe as Iago, me
as Desdemona, Paul as star of the show. Joe and I got Paul's
approval and we played the Shubert Theatre for two hundred
and ninety-six performances: the longest Shakespeare run
ever known on Broadway, after which we took the play on
a coast-to-coast tour. By then, a lot had changed between all
three of us.

INDIANAPOLIS

UTA *in a hotel bedroom, unpacking a suitcase.*

UTA. Have you no idea what I'm talking about?

> JOE, *who is out of sight in the bathroom, calls back to her:*

JOE. The water was running. What did you say?

UTA. There was an evening dress in the window of the store next door.

JOE. Why didn't I see it?

UTA. You were ringing the bell for the night-porter and he wasn't answering.

JOE. So what's it like?

UTA. It's an iridescent, sea-green, spangly dress. I've never seen one like it anywhere.

JOE. When would you wear a thing like that?

UTA. Parties, like tonight. Receptions, dinners. We've been to a whole stack of those and I feel dowdy as hell compared to the other women. I think I'll get it in the morning.

JOE. What'll it cost?

UTA. A hundred dollars.

> JOE *comes out of the bathroom.*

JOE. A hundred dollars? Are you serious?

UTA. I need to look good, Joe. I'm an actress. I'm on show.

JOE. I'm an actor and do you know what my tuxedo cost? Not to mention the shirt and shoes and the bow tie? Forty dollars the lot. One hundred dollars is ridiculous.

UTA. Don't worry! I'll pay for it!

JOE. What makes you think you can afford it?

UTA. Of course I can. I get the same as you.

JOE. We've got expenses, Uta. Do you know the interest on our loan? Do you know how many cheques I sent off this week? I don't want to argue about it. This was one of the most seriously annoying days of my life. Have you got any cigarettes? Give me your bag.

UTA. We smoked them all.

JOE. Shit.

Pause.

There's a machine in the lobby.

UTA. It's broken.

JOE. Dammit, I'm tired.

Pause.

UTA. Joe.

JOE. Mm-hm?

UTA. Why don't I know if I can afford a dress?

JOE. Not that again.

UTA. Why don't I even know if I've got a hundred dollars? Is that a stupid question?

JOE. It's not profoundly stupid, but I can't help wondering why you never asked it before.

UTA. Because it seems to me like…

JOE. Sweetheart, if you want to write our cheques and read the statements and the bills, you go right on ahead, nobody's stopping you. I'm just saving you the trouble.

UTA. It's no trouble, Joe, but it seems to me that it's only normal for an adult woman to know how much money she's got.

JOE. But with a married couple, one partner can take on certain responsibilities while the other partner takes on the rest of them. Have you ever wondered why you're on six hundred a week for the tour?

UTA. Isn't it what they offered?

JOE. *Au contraire*. I renegotiated. You'd be on three-fifty if I hadn't held out, and so would I. That's five hundred dollars a week more than we would have gotten without my efforts. So maybe you'll allow me some modest influence on the spending of it.

UTA. I didn't know about...

JOE. ...no, you didn't, because I didn't choose to brag about it. I also renegotiated our billing. You haven't objected to our names going above the title.

UTA. I don't give a damn where my name goes.

JOE. Well you ought to give a damn, because billing is status and status is money.

UTA. I don't give a damn about money either.

JOE. Yes, you do. You want a hundred dollars for a dress. Is that money or is it not?

The telephone rings.

UTA. That must be Paul.

JOE. Tell him we've got some rum up here if he wants to look in.

She answers the phone.

UTA. Hello? Oh, it's you!

(*To* JOE.) It's Peggy.

(*On the phone*.) No, we're wide awake, we've just arrived. It was a...

(*To* JOE.) She says can she come up?

JOE. Tell her it's okay.

UTA. That's fine. Room 824, just by the elevator.

Rings off.

Before she arrives...

JOE. I'm not gonna talk about this now.

UTA.…what's puzzling me is that I don't remember paying even one of my paycheques into a bank.

JOE. *I* pay them in. Have you only just noticed?

UTA. What do you pay them in to?

JOE. First American…

UTA. No, not which bank! Which bank *account*…?

JOE. Ours, sweetheart. Our bank account. Where else would the money go? Look, Peggy's coming up so…

UTA. Is it my bank account as well as yours?

JOE. Yes, in effect.

UTA. What *effect* are you talking about?

JOE. Oh, for God's sake, Uta…

UTA. Is my name printed at the bottom of the cheques?

JOE. No, why would it be? You don't write cheques. You've never written a cheque in your life.

UTA. So…

JOE. Listen to me. The name on the cheques is mine.

UTA. What, all of it?

JOE. What are you…?

Rather satirically, UTA *spells out his name to its full extent.*

UTA. 'José Vicente Ferrer de Otero y Cintrón?'

JOE. It says 'José Ferrer', okay? Because it's my account in a *technical* sense. Look, I don't want Peggy bursting in while we're…

UTA. So how come *my* paycheques end up in *your* bank account?

JOE. It's how it works, sweetie. I endorse them for you. On the back of the paycheque. Six hundred dollars, less deductions.

UTA. What do you write on the back of the paycheque?

JOE. What do you think? I write 'Uta fucking Hagen'. As a result of which, you get *use* of the money, which…

UTA. *You forge my signature!*

JOE. Uta, I do not…

UTA. You've got no right to do that!

JOE. It's purely a way of…

UTA. Week after week after week you have been… What kind of *idiot* do you think I am?

JOE. Good, fine, we'll change the system!

UTA. You call *that* a system?

JOE. Don't worry, it's all gonna be different! You pay the bills, you pay the carer, you pay the gardener, you get the roof fixed. Fuck it, Uta! Fuck it all! It's been a long fucking day and I am sick of it!

A knock on the door.

UTA. Let her in.

JOE. *You* let her in.

UTA *opens the door.* PEGGY *comes in. Slacks, shirt, cardigan.* UTA *and* JOE *are pleased enough to see her, but echoes of their row hang on in the air.*

PEGGY. Thank God, you've arrived. I've been so worried about the two of you. Joe, don't get up, you must be thoroughly worn out. I've brought some post for you from New York. Uta dear, I do hope there's nothing abusive. Some of the envelopes give one cause for alarm. Capital letters in green ink.

UTA. Give 'em to me.

She opens the letters, throwing the abusive ones away after a quick look.

PEGGY. They told me this is the best hotel in town, so I cannot imagine what the rest are like. The bar has been closed for hours. I don't suppose you have anything to drink?

JOE. We've got some rum for Paul.

PEGGY. Rum would be wonderful, thank you, Joe.

JOE *digs out the rum and pours some for* PEGGY. *Meanwhile:*

I've seen the theatre. The auditorium is a barn and the acoustic is appalling. The good news is that all performances are standing-room only. Packed to the rafters!

JOE. Let's hope they aren't planning to start a riot.

PEGGY. Why would they be?

JOE. This isn't England, Peggy. It's the USA and we're travelling south. This town's the northern headquarters of the Ku Klux Klan. Don't be surprised tomorrow night if the audience throws rocks at the stage when Paul starts smooching a white woman and feeling her up.

UTA. Oh, cut the melodrama.

(*To* PEGGY.) The audiences have been fine. It's when we walk out the stage door that the trouble starts.

JOE. Which is not so funny.

UTA. But it doesn't make us heroes. Okay, Joe?

There's an awkward pause, broken by PEGGY *and* JOE.

PEGGY. So…

JOE. So at dawn this morning, we're in Pittsburgh Airport, and what do we hear but, 'Paging Mr Paul Robeson and party.' So we shuffle our sleepy heads over to the desk, and it's 'Oh, we're sorry, but because of war priorities we can only offer you two tickets to Indianapolis for the three of you.'

PEGGY. Was it a racial thing?

UTA. It's always a racial thing.

JOE. She's right, it is. Paul looms over the guy and says 'Oh, that's too bad, we'll have to cancel the show, there'll be a scandal in the newspapers and what is your name, young man?' and after some further intimidation from him, they let us on, only it wasn't a direct flight…

UTA.… which nobody'd told us…

JOE.… so we stop in Dayton, Ohio and, after a long, long while, there's another announcement, 'Mr Robeson, will you come to the desk…'

PEGGY. Not again!

UTA. We couldn't believe it either.

JOE.… and this time there really were only two seats left.

UTA. I made them show me the plan.

JOE. She did. I say to Uta, 'You take the plane with Paul, I'll stay behind and either I'll find a later flight to Indianapolis or I'll take the train…

UTA.… and then reality butts in…

JOE.… because Paul declares, 'I am not crazy enough to arrive in Indianapolis with a white woman.'

PEGGY. Of course, of course…

UTA. So I propose that Paul and Joe take the plane, while I go look for…

JOE.… but I refuse to leave her alone in Dayton, Ohio…

UTA. Age of chivalry!

JOE.… only Paul can't stay there either, because the last time he was in Dayton he was involved in some nameless scandal and got run out of town…

UTA.… so now there's practically a fist-fight between the guys over who's gonna stay in Dayton to protect my maiden virtue…

JOE.… till we discover that there's a bus to Indianapolis leaving in thirty minutes.

UTA....so Paul gets a cab to the bus station...

JOE....and Uta and I land in Indianapolis to find a huge reception at the airport...

UTA....waiting for Paul, of course, not us...

JOE....but they swept us off to a party in a mansion...

UTA....it was *impressively* enormous, bandstand, marble swimming pool, flamingos...

JOE....where we hover about like idiots, till we hear that Paul has arrived at the bus station, so we go to collect him...

UTA....and it's back to the party...

JOE....big celebration, cheers, toasts...

UTA....Paul makes a speech...

JOE....Paul makes another speech and he naturally has to sing...

UTA....but we've been up since four-thirty this morning, so we're exhausted...

JOE....and we sneak away while nobody's looking. Paul's still there, I guess, singing 'Ol' Man River'.

UTA. Not in a thousand years. He hates that song.

She recites in parodic Southern States misery:

'Ah gits weary
An' sick of tryin'
Ah'm tired of livin'
An' skeered of dyin'...'

JOE. Bet you five bucks he sings it anyway.

UTA. Deal!

PEGGY. But Paul has arrived! He's here.

UTA. Where?

PEGGY. In his room, I imagine. I met him down in the lobby, checking in. I hope to God he gets some sleep. I hope we all do.

She gets up, about to go.

Thanks for the rum. In case you haven't got the call, it's six o'clock for a toddle around the stage, so you can sleep in.

There's a knocking at the door. JOE *opens it to* PAUL, *who holds up a key.*

JOE. Hi, pal. You okay?

PEGGY. Is your room all right?

PAUL. It isn't there.

PEGGY. What isn't?

PAUL. My room. It doesn't exist.

JOE. Where have you looked?

PAUL. Where have I looked, my friend? On the relevant floor, on the floor above and the floor below. You know what I think? I think I couldn't care less. I think I'll sleep on the floor right here.

PEGGY. Oh my God.

UTA. This is ridiculous.

JOE. Don't worry about it. I'll go down to the desk and create a scene. You coming, pal?

PAUL. I'll come and watch. But it's my firm belief that the aforesaid room is non-existent. Uta, it's good to see you. Take good care.

PAUL *and* JOE *go.*

PEGGY. Pray God it's a mistake.

UTA. Do you think it is?

PEGGY. No, I don't. I think the hotel is being vile. When I spoke to them from New York, they said they'd never had a Negro guest and they didn't want one now. I pulled every string in sight and I honestly thought they'd given in. But maybe they *did* give in and now they're having second thoughts at…

She looks at her watch.

…two in the morning. Where's that rum?

UTA. It's here.

PEGGY *pours for them both.*

Did you hear about the woman in Boston?

PEGGY. No, who was that?

UTA. Paul and I were coming down the elevator. I was rubbing
at a mark on his collar and a woman got in, nicely dressed,
perfectly normal-looking, and she took one look at us and
spat in my face. Bullseye. I didn't know what to do. I didn't
say a thing. I was too shocked.

PEGGY. What about Paul?

UTA. He didn't move. I was pressed up close to him because
of the woman, and he was like a rock of granite. He hardly
breathed.

PEGGY. God only knows what he was thinking.

UTA. I don't think anyone knows what he's thinking. Joe says
Paul has an overcoat with forty pockets, and the only person
who knows what's in them all is Paul himself.

PEGGY *is puzzled.*

It's a metaphor.

PEGGY. Well, he certainly baffles me.

One of them pours drinks.

Are you any happier in the show?

UTA. Why are you asking? You'll see it tomorrow night.

PEGGY. I'd like to hear it from you.

UTA. It's like it always was. I'm fine up to the second interval.
After that, I feel I'm faking it.

PEGGY. There are worse things than faking it some of the time.
Some actors fake it all the way through.

UTA. I don't like it. I feel pathetic. How can an intelligent woman love a man who treats her like that? He calls her a whore, he smothers her, and the last thing she says before she actually *dies* is 'Commend me to my kind lord.' I wish she'd say, 'Fuck you, Othello, I'm taking the next boat back to Venice.'

PEGGY. It's her background, darling, and the…

UTA. That's not the point. I need something I can use to make it real. Don't worry, I'll find it.

PEGGY. How is Paul?

UTA. Paul's the same.

PEGGY. And Joe?

UTA. Joe is brilliant but he keeps adding stuff. He's overdecorating.

PEGGY. It is a great temptation of that part to be too clever. You should have seen Larry Olivier as Iago. Full of tricks!

She relaxes into her chair and holds out her glass for more rum.

Iago is not a gloating Machiavel. He's a down-to-earth professional soldier who thinks that Othello has slept with his wife.

She quotes with colourful bravura:

'I do suspect the lusty Moor
Hath leap'd into my seat; the thought whereof
Doth, like a poisonous mineral, gnaw my inwards.'

He's in the grip of that terrifying madness that we call physical jealousy. I think we're all quite prone to it at times, don't you agree?

UTA. Why are you bringing that up?

PEGGY. I think you know.

UTA. Yeah, maybe I do, but…

PEGGY. Of course I hate to interfere, but as director of the show, I do need to know about any personal issues that might be disruptive. Am I right in thinking that the affair is still going on?

Pause.

Am I?

UTA. How do you know about it?

PEGGY. It's perfectly obvious.

UTA. Is it?

PEGGY. Yes, they've hardly kept it secret.

UTA. What? Who are you talking about?

PEGGY. Joe and Bianca, of course. Who did you think I meant?

UTA. Oh, nobody else.

PEGGY. Is there anything I can do to help?

UTA. Like what?

PEGGY. We could replace Bianca. Couldn't be easier. She's only got two scenes and she's not very good.

UTA. Lose her, you'll lose Joe.

PEGGY. Oh, nonsense! Joe is having a huge success in a marvellous role. He wouldn't dream of giving it up for a dim little actress. I could speak to him, of course, and warn him that…

UTA. No, don't do that.

Pause.

I've always known what Joe is like. I can't complain about him now. It would be stupid.

The door opens. JOE *and* PAUL *are there.*

PEGGY. Did you find the room? Is it all right?

PAUL. I've gotta book to read.

He sits and reads a book.

UTA. Joe?

JOE. The desk clerk led us up to the mezzanine, through the laundry, through the kitchens, down some poky stairs where we discover not a suite, or even a room, but a minute little office with a canvas bed and a fan on a table.

PEGGY. No bathroom?

JOE. Not even a basin. I said, very politely, 'This room is unsuitable for Mr Robeson,' and we came back here.

PEGGY. Good God.

UTA. I'm out of here. I'm not gonna stay one minute longer.

JOE. Nor me.

PEGGY. But where do we go?

UTA. Another hotel.

PEGGY. It's two in the morning.

For a moment they are flummoxed. Then PAUL *speaks up from his quiet corner of the room.*

PAUL. Back to the party. To the flamingo place. I know the lady who owns it.

UTA. How the hell do you know her?

PAUL. Doesn't matter. She'll be thrilled. Her staff will make up big, soft beds and, in the morning, we'll have breakfast on the patio and a dip in the pool.

JOE. Good thinking, pal.

(*To* UTA.) Let's pack.

UTA. You call for a cab.

PEGGY. I'll see you all in the lobby in ten minutes!

JOE. Say, Paul?

PAUL. What, pal?

JOE. Uta and I have got five bucks on whether you sang 'Ol' Man River' at the party tonight.

PEGGY

PEGGY. Following morning. Brisk walk. Typical Midwest town with a real cigar-store Indian on the sidewalk. I give my talk: 'The Director's View of Othello'. The largely female audience strikes a decorous note in linen suits, straw hats and permanent waves. They ask the same old question and I reply as always: 'No, madam, Othello is not a lightly bronzed Arabian of the kind familiar to us from *The Desert Song*. He is an *African* and will be played as such by the great star of radio, stage and screen, Paul Robeson.' Some hands are clamorous in applause, some stay firmly folded on their owners' laps.

I see the show. The supporting men are adequate for wartime. Joe good but flashy, Emilia dull, Uta much improved, as always. But it's Paul I have come to see. And, oh, his acting! I despair. Othello mustn't *intone*! He mustn't *boom*! He mustn't sound like an old ham actor, or a gloomy preacher warning his congregation about the perils of drink. His words would reach our hearts and upset us dreadfully, because they would be *spontaneous*. They'd be *real*. Never have I had such a failure with an actor and God knows I've had a few. After the show, I had a thousand notes for him, but I feebly winnowed them down to three and he didn't want *those*. Walking back to my hotel, I ponder a universal truth of theatre: a woman directing a play needs the manipulative guile of Elizabeth the First, Lucrezia Borgia and Cleopatra to make any impression whatsoever!

On the plane, surprisingly, the image returns to me of Uta rubbing at a mark on Paul's collar. I wonder if that dreadful woman had noticed something about those two that I had missed.

CLEVELAND

PAUL *alone, half-in, half-out of bed, talking to someone who's in the bathroom.*

PAUL. It's the silence. It's the stillness. I sing the last note of a song and there's a beat of astonishment before they applaud. That's how I know I've got them. Or I speak at a rally and I feel them here…

He gestures with cupped hands.

…like that. Communion. Them and me. But this acting thing just plain eludes me. Every night I hear the audience losing interest. Cough cough here, cough cough there. Little heads jiggling from side to side. Maybe they're happy enough because they paid to see Paul Robeson and there I am, but *I'm* not happy. I hoped that Peggy would be some help, what with her Shakespeare background, but she's disappointed me. Last week in Indianapolis, I said to her, 'Peggy, don't assume I've got some natural unspoiled quality that can't be tampered with. I *want* to be tampered with. Teach me! Make me a good actor!'

UTA *comes out of the bathroom wearing* PAUL*'s dressing gown.*

UTA. What did she say?

PAUL. She said, 'Stress this word more.' 'Stress that word less.' I said, 'Peggy, this is superficial. What am I missing?' 'Fine,' she says, 'Act Five. Othello is killing Desdemona. I want to *see* his rage. I want to *feel* it.'

UTA. So you said…

PAUL. I said, 'Peggy, I spend a major part of my life trying *not* to be in a rage.'

UTA. What did she do?

PAUL. Went back to New York. Left me high and dry. What do I do? You tell me.

UTA. Can I make a suggestion?

PAUL. Make it.

But she senses some reserve.

UTA. Do you *want* me to?

PAUL. That's what I said.

UTA. Try this exercise.

PAUL. I'm waiting.

UTA. Think of something in the past that made you angry.

PAUL. Have I got to do this?

UTA. I think you do.

PAUL. Like that woman in the elevator?

UTA. No, she's no good. It's gotta be a time when you didn't *suppress* your anger. When it *exploded*.

PAUL. That's gonna take me a long way back.

UTA. So go there.

PAUL. All the way back to college?

UTA. If that's where it happened.

PAUL. Just to paint the picture, it was near as dammit an all-white institution. Just me and one black brother, both on the football team.

UTA. Go on.

PAUL. I've made a tackle and I'm flat on the ground with my right palm spread out like that.

His hand is flat on her body.

UTA. Like that?

PAUL. Wouldn't you rather we were doing something else?

UTA. I can wait.

PAUL. One of the white guys comes running over and he stamps on my hand, hard as he can. Scoops off every one of my fingernails.

UTA is horrified.

UTA. What!

PAUL. So I…

UTA. Wait! Let me get over that.

Her eyes closed, she breathes deeply.

Jesus. Okay. Show me what you did.

PAUL demonstrates, putting great energy into what he's doing. But he's telling the story, not living the moment.

PAUL. I lifted that player up. I saw the blood running down my arm. I held him high in the air. I felt no weight from him. I was possessed. If the coach hadn't stopped me, I would have smashed that bastard down…

He throws down the imaginary player.

'…with all my force and *roared* with anger.'

He roars. Then waits for her reaction.

So?

UTA. Now do it with feeling.

PAUL. I just did.

UTA. No, you didn't. You pulled a furious face and you yelled so loud they could hear you across the street. But it was phoney, Paul. It wouldn't have scared Desdemona and it didn't scare me. It wasn't coming from there.

She touches his heart.

Or there.

She touches his groin.

Why don't we try again later?

PAUL. Up to you.

She gets into bed.

Is Joe a good actor?

UTA. What?

PAUL. Is Joe…?

UTA. I heard you. What's that got to do with anything?

PAUL. Tell me.

UTA. He's a fabulous actor.

PAUL. Better than me?

UTA. You're different people. Joe is an actor through and
through. It's what he lives for. Why do you act?

PAUL. Same reason I sing. It gives me a platform. People see
me and they know who I am and they hear what I've got to
say. What's wrong with that?

UTA. Nothing's *wrong*. It's just that every afternoon you do
a benefit, or a rally and you arrive at the theatre exhausted.
Then you walk on stage still thinking about equality or racial
prejudice, because what you believe, deep down, is that
plays are just ridiculous nonsense compared to important
stuff like that. I love you for thinking that way. You're a
great man. But you can't be a great man and also be a great
actor. Not at the same time! If you want to be like Joe,
you've gotta ditch the rest of your life. But you're not gonna
do that, and I don't want you to. I prefer you as you are.

PAUL. Even though my acting's not so hot?

UTA. I don't care about that.

He looks at her with wonder as though for the first time.

PAUL. Has it ever occurred to you that we could get married?

UTA. Essie would never let you go.

PAUL. You're right, she wouldn't. But Joe would get over it
fast enough. Come here.

UTA. No.

She moves away from him.

PAUL. What's the matter?

UTA. You put me off by saying 'Joe'. I think he might suspect us. It's making me nervous.

PAUL. When did this start?

UTA. After Buffalo.

PAUL. What happened there?

UTA. I had a scare.

PAUL. A what?

UTA. I was late. I thought I might be pregnant.

PAUL. Jesus Christ!

UTA. Don't get excited! I wasn't. I took the test and it was negative. So we…

PAUL. Did Joe know you were having this test?

UTA. It was his idea. That's why we rushed it through. He seemed anxious. I thought he was worrying that I'd have to leave the tour. Or that *both* of us would. But now I wonder whether…

PAUL. No, no, no! Let's get some logic into this! Who did Joe think had caused this pregnancy?

UTA. There wasn't a…

PAUL. *If* there had been one? *Who* did he think was the father?

UTA. Himself, I guess.

PAUL. You *guess*?

UTA. That's what I mostly think. But…

PAUL *freezes, radiating a quiet, controlled fury.*

Paul, what are you doing?

PAUL. I'm not doing anything.

UTA. Yes, you are. You're doing that silent thing, like you did in the elevator.

PAUL. You told me… no, you swore… that you and Joe don't
sleep together.

UTA. We don't. Not as a rule.

PAUL *explodes*.

PAUL. Then this makes no fucking sense! How could he
imagine for one moment that…?

UTA. I said, 'as a rule'. I didn't say never. Have you got that?

PAUL *is stunned by this new idea*.

PAUL. Sure.

UTA. So…

PAUL. What would you have done if the test were positive?

UTA. I hadn't decided.

PAUL. You mean you might have had the child?

UTA. I would want to, yes.

PAUL. What about your career?

UTA. My career's irrelevant.

PAUL. That's not true.

UTA. I care about acting, Paul. It's an art. It's only Broadway
ingénues have a career.

PAUL. Don't be naïve. With that baby in your arms, you
wouldn't get an acting job anywhere in this country.

UTA. Bullshit. I've got a four-year-old daughter and I've never
been out of work since she was born.

PAUL. That's not the same. This child would make you
unemployable. I wouldn't allow you to take the risk.

UTA. What risk? It isn't…

She stops.

Oh, my God. No, Paul, it isn't like that. If there *had* been
a baby, it would have been Joe's.

PAUL *struggles to take this in.*

PAUL. Not Joe's for sure?

UTA. Yes, Joe's quite definitely.

PAUL. You know this because…?

UTA. I know when it was. It was that split week in Flint,
Michigan. Joe and that poop Bianca were fighting. You and
I hadn't been seeing each other because of that woman in
Grand Rapids. I was upset about my marriage. So Joe and
I… Do you want me to spell it out?

PAUL. Was it just that once, this 'Joe and you'?

UTA. It was just that *week*. I'm sorry I gave you the wrong idea.
I'm no good at this. I've never been unfaithful to Joe, not in
six years of marriage.

PAUL. Sleeping with me doesn't count?

UTA. Not as being unfaithful.

PAUL. Why not?

UTA. Because I love you.

Pause.

Are you angry?

PAUL. No.

UTA. Not jealous about Joe, are you?

PAUL. How could I be? Lovers don't have that privilege. Joe's
your husband and I love him. I love you both. Thank you for
telling me. I need to shower.

He moves to the bathroom.

UTA. When you're done, shall we try that exercise again?

PAUL. No, I don't think so.

He goes out.

JOE

JOE. Ten months ago. Shubert Theatre, West 44th Street. Outside her dressing-room door, I pause to knock. 'Hello, it's me.' But a barely audible sound from inside the room tells me...

Pause.

...that if I open that door it will bring disaster. Back in my dressing room, I look in the mirror. That's what it means to be an actor, that the first thing you do when you know your wife is cheating on you, is to wonder, 'What do I look like?' And then, 'How can I use it?' Over the basin, as I splash cold water on my face, it dawns on me that the revelation I've just had, is, in reality, a host of small revelations opening up like tiny windows in an advent calendar. The time they both came late to rehearsal, but he dallied outside to mask his arrival. The scent of his aftershave in a hotel room. Her afternoon at the races when there were no races. The trip to a New York art exhibit when, like some weird example of déjà vu by proxy, it became clear to me that she'd seen it the day before. On a windy sidewalk, I gaze up at our window and wonder how to get back inside. Do I call the room? Will she be there? Will he be there? Should I warn them by whistling a tune as I come out the elevator?

Iago only suspected it. *I know.*

WINNIPEG

JOE *alone*. PAUL *at the door*.

PAUL. Hi, Joe!

JOE. Come in, pal.

> PAUL *comes in*.

PAUL. Nice big room you got here. You ought to see mine.

JOE. Oh, don't tell me, another fuck-up!

PAUL. No, this is Canada, baby! My room's palatial. Robeson is in clover. Double bed the size of a barn door. You want a game?

JOE. I was gonna go out.

PAUL. Stay and play.

JOE. Why not?

> PAUL *tips chess pieces out of the box and lays them out. Meanwhile:*

> I slept in late. Had breakfast sent up.

PAUL. I woke at dawn. Went for a stroll by the river. It'll be Christmas soon. Hey, that was a nice audience last night.

JOE. It was a good show.

PAUL. Glad you think so. I felt happier than I've done for a while. I wasn't so *laden*. Not so ponderous. Know why that is, Joe? Because that monstrous cycle of oppression doesn't exist here like it does in the USA. Like when I first stepped off the plane in the Soviet Union. That's the real 'Land of the Free'.

JOE. Oh yeah?

PAUL. You can take that sceptical look off of your face. I'm gonna go back to Moscow when the war is over. You ought to come too. Be an education for you.

JOE. I wouldn't enjoy it, Paul. I read too much about the show trials and the killing of people who happen to speak out of turn.

PAUL. Then you should ask yourself who owns the newspapers that print those stories. The press is a rich man's club. I'm not claiming that the Soviet Union is perfection. It's a new society. Mistakes will happen, but they're not systematic, like those same mistakes would be in the USA, because the Soviet system is a good one. Where's Uta got to?

JOE. She went out while I was asleep. You didn't see her?

PAUL. No. Oh, there's a piece in the local paper. *Winnipeg Tribune*. Says she acted the two of us off the stage last night. You seen it?

JOE. You know I don't read reviews.

PAUL. Uta's gonna cut it out to stick it in her scrapbook.

He holds out his closed fists.

Choose.

JOE. How do you know if you haven't seen her?

PAUL. She... sticks *all* her good reviews into her scrapbook. When it's full, she sends it to old Papa Hagen. Hell, you know that.

JOE. I need to take a leak.

He goes into the bathroom. PAUL *stays, in full knowledge of the mistake he's made. He erupts, but quietly so as not to be heard.*

PAUL. *Shit!*

JOE *comes back and chooses* PAUL's *left hand: white.*

You okay?

JOE. I'm fine.

PAUL. You to play.

JOE *plays.*

I never thought I would take up acting until, one day, my boss called me into his office. He said, 'Robeson, if you intend to be a lawyer, you ought to know that you will never represent a white client of ours in court, because he will not trust a Negro to win his case.' That was *enough*! I shook the dust of that company from my feet and then, lucky for me, a couple of plays came along that called for a man of colour in the leading role.

He plays.

JOE. Eugene O'Neill.

He plays.

PAUL. The very man. Then people decided that I can sing and the rest you know.

JOE. Your move.

PAUL *plays.*

PAUL. Is this tour working out for you okay?

JOE. It's a great experience. Every night I find some new aspect of my character.

He plays.

PAUL. You sound like a schoolteacher, Joe!

JOE. I can't help that. I try to keep my performance fresh and I hope I do.

PAUL. I'm only kidding. Who is that critic anyway? Some young punk who wanted a free ticket, I suppose.

He plays.

JOE. I don't care who he is. Forget it.

PAUL. Sure.

JOE *plays.*

Not mad at me, are you?

JOE. Why should I be?

PAUL. No reason that I can think of.

JOE. Neither can I.

PAUL. That's good, that's good.

He plays, sneaking a thoughtful look at JOE *before speaking.*

Has there been anything new in your life lately?

JOE. Nothing you don't know about.

He plays.

PAUL. Have you ever thought you might not make it till the end of the tour?

JOE. What's that?

PAUL *plays.*

PAUL. I wondered if you thought you'd...

JOE. I heard you. Why would I not make it? What do you mean?

PAUL. It's a long engagement. Six months more to go.

JOE. I gotta contract, Paul.

PAUL. You could get out of it if you wanted.

JOE. Which I don't.

PAUL. What about Uta?

JOE. Uta and I are a team. If I stay, she stays. What's this about anyway?

PAUL. It's not about anything, Joe.

JOE. Look, I know there's been some talk about firing Bianca. She was very distressed. I challenged Peggy about it and she climbed down. But she never said anything about losing me and Uta.

PAUL. Of course she didn't! She'd be broken-hearted! So would I. I wouldn't allow it.

JOE. Glad to hear it.

He plays.

PAUL. Only life is unpredictable.

JOE. How?

PAUL. Things can change.

JOE. *How* would they change?

PAUL improvises a reason.

PAUL. Let's say, if Uta were to get some very attractive
Hollywood offer.

He plays.

JOE. She won't.

PAUL. Why not?

JOE. She's got the wrong kind of face. The camera likes small-
boned features, like a bird. And Puerto Rican character-actors
tend not to become movie stars, so you're stuck with me
as well.

He plays.

PAUL. That's excellent, Joe. It's what I hoped.

He relaxes, accepting that further information about JOE
and UTA*'s relationship won't be forthcoming. He plays.*

Any idea what's coming up for you afterwards?

JOE. Uta and I will go back home and stick our lives together.
You've seen our house in Ossining.

PAUL. Beautiful place.

JOE. We're building an apple orchard. Different varieties every
tree. All traditional. Uta's family had one back in Germany, so
her old man tells me. We'll eat home-grown and shop at the
farmers' market. Saturday nights, we'll entertain. We can sleep
ten. Midnight strikes, headlights through the window, crunch
of tyres on the gravel. Actor friends coming down from New
York. Late supper, charades, songs round the piano.

He plays.

The kids are sitting halfway up the stairs…

PAUL *frowns*.

PAUL. I thought you only had one kid.

JOE. I have a daughter and I love her. But I want a son. I need a son. It's the Latino in me.

PAUL. My son and I are strangers.

He plays.

I blame his mother. What a snob! She's built a house so awful I can hardly stand to walk through the door. A make-believe Deep South mansion, pillars across the front, you expect to see Clark Gable carrying Scarlett O'Hara up the stairs. If there's anything I despise, it's the black middle-class copying their one-time masters. My father was born a slave.

JOE. So I've read.

He plays.

PAUL. Every time I tell a journalist that, I wonder if I'm truly honouring him, or whether I'm grabbing a little authenticity for myself.

JOE. You're honouring him.

PAUL. He fled to the north as a kid and in time he became a pastor. The elders fired him on account of the radical content of his sermons, so he did menial jobs until he could start his own little church. And there he flourished. He never went back on what he believed. Couldn't do it. He was poor and I am rich, but I wish I was sustained by faith like that man was.

He plays.

JOE. I have people of colour in my family.

PAUL *stares at him in surprise*.

PAUL. You do?

JOE. *Extended* family.

PAUL. Strange people they must be.

JOE. Why?

PAUL. Because I don't recall their coming to see you in the show.

JOE. They live back home.

PAUL. In Puerto Rico? What do they do there?

JOE. It doesn't matter.

He plays. PAUL *is curious and uneasy:*

PAUL. Why don't you tell me about this extended family of yours?

He plays.

JOE. I just did.

PAUL. Tell me more.

JOE. They cut cane in my family's sugar plantations.

He plays.

PAUL. Is that your way of saying that they're descended from slaves?

JOE. You could put it like that.

PAUL. Your family's slaves?

He plays. JOE *shrugs.*

From the days when great-granddaddy Ferrer could rape any young lady of colour who took his fancy?

JOE. I never said anyone got raped.

PAUL. Oh, are you claiming the slave-women could refuse the advances of their masters?

JOE. I never said that either. It was a long time ago.

He plays.

PAUL. A very long time. Only a crazy person would hate you for it.

With anger stirring inside him, he stares at JOE.

JOE. Are you gonna play, or are you gonna go on looking at me like that?

PAUL. I'll play.

He plays, tense.

Can I ask you a question of an intimate nature?

JOE. Ask it.

PAUL. Flint, Michigan. Remember it?

JOE. Rich audience.

Confidently, he plays.

So many fur coats they couldn't all fit in the cloakroom. What about it?

PAUL. I recall that you and Bianca weren't so close that week.

JOE. Bianca comes and goes.

PAUL plays.

I hope you're not being critical of my private life.

PAUL exhibits bonhomie.

PAUL. Jesus, Joe, I'm in no position to cast the first stone! I only wondered...?

JOE. Bianca threw a tantrum for a coupla days. It was nothing that a bit of affection couldn't put right.

He plays.

Why do you ask? Do you have your eye on her?

PAUL. I would never do that. Bianca is your woman.

He plays.

JOE. How ethical of you.

PAUL. Still, I guess it worked out well for you and Uta.

JOE. *What?*

PAUL. I'm only thinking that, with Bianca out of the way, Uta and you must have gotten a lot closer, man and wife.

JOE. Jesus, Paul! Do you think my love-life's like the fucking weather house? The little sunny person comes out and the little rainy person goes back in?

PAUL. It's only that…

JOE. Uta and I are a happily married couple in every sense of the word.

He plays.

PAUL. Oh, sure, I…

JOE. She is a highly sensuous woman.

PAUL. I don't doubt it.

JOE. Whatever I do, however I roam, we slake our marital appetites throughout the year. You must have heard us through the walls in some of those cheap hotels.

PAUL starts at him in shock.

Your move.

Distracted, PAUL *makes a bad move. He mutters his frustration.*

Take it back if you want.

PAUL. Why's there no air in this room?

He goes to a window and opens it. A violent wind blows in.

JOE. Fuck, Paul! It's freezing!

PAUL returns to the chessboard. Both men are very cold.

PAUL. I needed to breathe. Your play.

JOE moves a piece.

JOE. Check.

UTA

UTA. I never stopped believing that Paul could be a good actor. What didn't he have, that an actor needs? And he wasn't the man to give up easily so, week after week, on those long afternoons, when any self-respecting adulterous couple would have been taking a well-earned rest, Paul and I went through Othello's character, his status, his motivations, his super-objective and even his line-readings! This was the start of my love of teaching, by the way. But however much better I thought he'd got, when it came to the show that night, he was phoney as hell. I wonder now if the yielding-up, the sharing of self with the self of another, which is so much a part of acting, was beyond the reach of a man as stubborn as Paul. Because stubborn is what he was. If you wanted to put a name to his heroic flaw, that might have been it. Although another flaw of his was less heroic, as I was soon to find.

SEATTLE

Night. Dark room. A noise.

UTA. Who's that?

PAUL. It's Paul.

UTA. Christ, Paul, what are you...? I'm putting the light on.

She does, then opens the door. PAUL *is there.*

What're you doing in Seattle?

PAUL. I'm here for the show.

UTA. The show doesn't open till Monday, Paul. You're four days early.

PAUL. I know, I know. I had a concert tonight. Anti-lynching.

UTA. How'd it go?

He comes in.

PAUL. It was good in the hall. But there were people outside.

UTA. Doing what?

PAUL. Protesting.

UTA. Against lynching?

PAUL. No, against me! They were holding up placards. 'Robeson traitor to the USA.' While I'm speaking out for the safety and lives of US citizens.

UTA. Just a handful of cranks who don't like you.

PAUL. Maybe, maybe, but a word like 'traitor' don't go away so easy. It hangs in the air like a rotten smell. I walked back here in a troubled mood and the clerk at the desk said you'd arrived. I didn't expect you here so early. Why's Joe not with you?

UTA. He'll be here Monday. We got flooded over Christmas.
I'd had enough of leaves and blocked-up gutters, so I took an
early flight. Paul, you and I have got to talk.

PAUL. Is something wrong?

UTA. When I was...

PAUL. If I'm in trouble, I wanna keep it till the morning.

UTA. I won't get any sleep with it on my mind. It's got to come
out. Sit down.

PAUL. I'm fine as I am.

UTA. So this is it. I was doing some Christmas shopping in
New York and I had an hour to spare, so I called on Freda.
I'd left a scarf at her house one time.

PAUL. The house on Bleecker Street?

UTA. Yes, Paul, the house where you and I had our little
assignations.

PAUL. Why're you being sarcastic? Was Freda not nice to you?

UTA. She was nice up to a point.

PAUL. Uh-huh?

UTA. She opened a bottle of wine and we chatted around the
kitchen table. Then the topic of conversation turned to you.
She said...

She stops.

PAUL. Am I gonna like this?

UTA. You tell me. She said, 'Now Paul's away on tour, at least
I can enjoy a good night's sleep.'

PAUL. That could mean a lot of things.

UTA. I thought so too, so I asked her what meant and, well, she
didn't need much encouragement. I guess you know what
she was aiming at.

PAUL *can guess*.

PAUL. Jesus.

UTA. She wanted to tell me about your affair.

PAUL. Well, Freda's and my affair, if that's what you wanna call it, was way in the past, so it's not worth getting...

UTA. You're a liar, Paul! It was going on all the time that we were seeing each other in New York. Because I asked her and she told me! Can you imagine how humiliated I felt...?

PAUL. There was no need for you to...

UTA. ...and then it all came back to me in glorious Technicolor. I'd ring the bell, she'd come to the door, looking all homey with flour up her arms, and then she'd watch the two of us going upstairs, thinking, 'How can that fool of an actress not know that he fucked me last night?'

PAUL. You don't know what she was thinking.

UTA. I'm an actress, Paul! I have insight into people! That's my job! I am so fucking angry with you!

PAUL. This is not what you think it is.

UTA. Oh no?

PAUL. No, not at all.

UTA. Are you...?

PAUL. Freda and I go back many years. Both as friends and as, as, political workers...

UTA. Oh, for...!

PAUL. ...and she's a lonely woman. She sees me as some kind of rock of security, I imagine, and...

UTA. And what? You tell me what!

PAUL. ...she needs support from time to time. I don't know why you're so surprised...

UTA. I'm surprised because...

PAUL. ...because, in my opinion, the situation was obvious to...

UTA.…It *would* be obvious to anyone with an ounce of worldly wisdom. It just wasn't obvious to me.

PAUL. Well, if Freda is the only reason that you're mad at me, I need to…

UTA.…if she *was* I'd be *less* mad, but…

PAUL.…but what?

UTA.…but then she started a run-down on your entire New York love-life.

PAUL. Jesus, no! Why did you let her?

UTA. I wanted to know! I couldn't tear myself away! I was sitting there open-mouthed!

PAUL. So what did she say?

UTA. Where shall I start? She made a joke about that rich bitch who hosted the Halloween gala…

PAUL.…who you already know about, because you've sniped about her often enough…

UTA.…you bet I've sniped…

PAUL.…although I've never denied it…

UTA.…and then that tweedy journalist from *Variety*…

PAUL. Who? No, that's absurd.

UTA. Are you denying it?

PAUL. No, I'm not, because if I deny it you're just gonna invent some other damn woman. Why are we even talking like this? I thought you and I were above this kinda…

UTA. Paul, I liked that *Variety* journalist. We talked for half an hour. It's just so creepy and disgusting to find out that…

PAUL. I did not sleep with…

UTA. No, listen to me! I don't own you. You don't own me. We know that. That is fine. So if some stupid little jaunt on the side is gonna make you feel good, who cares? It doesn't matter to me. But when there are more and more of these, and suddenly there's a girl in every port, I wonder what the fuck is going on? What are you doing? And what are you trying to say? Because it's clear as daylight that you don't respect these women, and you don't respect me either.

PAUL. Are you finished? 'Cause I'll level with you now...

UTA. ...glad to hear it...

PAUL. ...but I'm not gonna trudge through some endless list of real or mythical women I may have met at some time or another. All I will say, and this is important...

UTA. Tell me.

PAUL. ...so listen closely...

UTA. Say it!

PAUL. ...you have more power to hurt me than any woman I've ever known.

UTA *struggles to take this in*.

UTA. What?

PAUL. You heard what I said.

UTA. *Me* hurt *you*?

PAUL. Yes, *you* hurt *me*! If you can't see that not one of these women you're getting so stressed about means a fraction of what you mean to me, then you are hurtful and cruel and superficial. That is the truth. Why don't we throw this bullshit gossip out of the window? Because there's only one thing that matters, and that is trust.

UTA. Have you any idea how upsetting it is, to find that someone you *thought* you could trust is...?

PAUL. It's not 'upsetting'!

UTA. What?

PAUL *explodes, burning with real anger*.

PAUL. It is not *upsetting*, because that word is *not enough*! Try *'devastating'*. Try night after night drowning in delusional speculations. Try feeling that the whole of your personality is being *deformed* and *twisted*.

UTA. What are you talking about? You've lost me.

PAUL. Are you truthful?

UTA. What?

PAUL. Do you tell me the truth?

UTA. Yes, I do.

PAUL. You said you got an early flight because of leaves and gutters and shit like that.

UTA. And so?

PAUL. That wasn't true. You took that flight because of what Freda told you.

UTA. What if I did?

PAUL. Why did you lie?

UTA. This is insane! I'm *not* in the wrong. I don't want to talk to you when you're like this. Leave me alone.

She moves away from him. He tries to collect himself.

PAUL. Uta.

UTA. What?

PAUL. I'm trying to talk to you.

UTA. So go ahead.

PAUL. Do you remember Winnipeg?

UTA. *What?*

PAUL. We took a walk by the river…

UTA. Why're we talking about that now?

PAUL.…because that is where the nightmare started. I called on Joe for a game of chess. With joy in my heart. Because you and

I had just made love in a bed the size of a barn door. I made a slip of the tongue about the local paper. Then it began.

UTA. What did?

PAUL. The doubt. The eating-away. The undercutting.

UTA. Not by Joe.

PAUL. All by Joe. He said his family had been slave-owners.

UTA. You can't blame people for what happened in the past.

PAUL. Oh no? What if those long-dead slaves paid for Joe all the way through Princeton?

UTA. What's this got to do with you and me?

PAUL. Joe had one reason only to rub my nose in a thing like that. It was to kill the love between us.

UTA. I don't believe it.

PAUL. There's more. He told me about your place in Ossining. Moonlit countryside. Midnight hour. A crunch of tyres and a beam of headlights sweeping across the room. Broadway actors. Cocktails, charades, sophisticated chatter.

UTA. Just what is the point of…?

PAUL. For Christ's sake, isn't it plain as daylight? Why would he paint that charming, bohemian, bourgeois, smug fucking scene, if not to make clear that I don't belong in it?

UTA. Do you *want* to belong in it?

PAUL. No, I don't! But I don't want to be the little boy on the staircase who's being kept out.

UTA. What little boy? There *is* no boy.

PAUL. The boy is the heart of it. The boy is the clue. The boy Joe wants. The son he wants.

UTA. Every man wants a son.

PAUL. No, he was telling me something else.

UTA. What?

PAUL freezes: he's entered his dangerous state of suppressed rage.

Why are you looking at me like that?

PAUL. Are you still pretending you don't know?

UTA. I have no idea.

PAUL's rage begins to spill out and grow.

PAUL. You're a fake. You're a liar.

UTA. How dare you say that?

PAUL. You have been lying to me and lying and lying and lying.

UTA. I have not!

PAUL. You're planning a kid.

UTA. I'm not!

PAUL. You and Joe are planning a kid and you've been lying to me.

UTA. I'm not! I'm not!

PAUL. It's true as I'm standing here! I got it from Joe!

UTA. I don't believe you!

PAUL. You've been sleeping with him all through this tour. All through New York. He told me!

UTA. It's a lie! He'd never have said that!

PAUL. You've been laughing at me! You've been treating me like a fool!

UTA. Joe doesn't lie! He'd never have laughed at you!

PAUL. I hear your noises through the walls, in every cheap hotel…

UTA. You're making it up!

PAUL....I've heard bedsprings, I've heard floorboard-creaks and footsteps...

UTA. Old buildings! There are noises all the time!

PAUL....I was so dumb. I was an idiot...

UTA. Will you calm down?

PAUL....I've tried to write those noises off as nothing...

UTA. Listen to me, you madman! If Joe and I are sleeping together, which we are *not*, what the *fuck* right have you got to complain about it? You of all people. After you and Freda...

PAUL. Why are we still talking about Freda?

UTA. Because it *started* with Freda! I was on the plane out here, trying to straighten out this garbage in my head, and, out of nowhere, I thought, 'But that was only in *New York*. What about on tour...?'

PAUL. Stop this! Stop this!

UTA....and all those women I've been noticing, month after month, thinking 'Oh, who might *she* be?' and 'What's *that* old broad doing backstage?', suddenly leapt into life before my eyes like a fucking freak show...

PAUL. I don't wanna hear this!

UTA. The redhead in Detroit. The classics lecturer in Ann Arbor.

PAUL. No. No.

UTA. What about the union-organiser in Cincinnati. Did you sleep with her the night she 'missed her train'?

PAUL. What makes you think...?

UTA. *Did* you?

PAUL. Yes. I've known her for fifteen years. Why's that so...?

UTA. What about the singer who'd been on your gospel tour?

PAUL. Maybe I did, on the gospel tour, three years ago.

UTA. The flamingo-woman in Indianapolis?

PAUL. No! No! Why're you yelling at me?

UTA. Because I'm furious at your lies!

PAUL. I do not lie.

UTA. You lied about Freda.

PAUL. Freda, yes, because I knew you'd misinterpret what she and I…

UTA. You lied about the woman in Cincinnati!

She hits him.

PAUL (*controlled*). Don't do that, Uta.

UTA. How do I know you didn't sleep with that *Variety* woman?

She hits him.

You didn't deny it! You *can't* deny it.

PAUL (*controlled*). I just did.

UTA. I *trusted* her. She had *integrity.*

PAUL. Jesus Christ! I did not sleep with her! I *could* have done and I wouldn't have minded…

UTA. How do I know that? How do I know?

She hits him again. He moves away from her.

PAUL. Uta, if you go on hitting me, something bad's gonna happen.

UTA. Tell me the truth! Tell me the truth!

PAUL. I have done, dammit!

UTA. Liar!

PAUL *charges across the room and grabs her.*

Stop that! You're hurting!

PAUL. You deceived me! You betrayed me! You whore!

He seizes a pillow and tries to press it over her face.

UTA. Take it away! I can't breathe!

He presses the pillow over her face. It seems that his entire intention is to kill her. Then sanity returns. He recoils from her in horror. Silence for a moment. Then:

PAUL. Uta, baby! I'm so sorry! I'm so sorry!

They stare at each other in amazement.

What did I do?

PEGGY

PEGGY. Remember *The Lady Vanishes*? The Hitchcock film in
which a little old lady gets kidnapped by the Nazis? That was
my mother. Dame May Whitty. A difficult mother in a way.
Yet where would I be without her? When I was six years old,
she pushed me on to the stage at the Albert Hall, so that in
future years I could say I'd trodden the boards with Ellen
Terry. When John Barrymore brought his *Hamlet* to London,
she got me the part of a waiting-woman so I could watch him
every night. It is to her that I owe my eye for acting, which is
what I live by now. It's my bread and butter. That's what
made it so very odd, a couple of weeks after Christmas,
when I saw *Othello* again. There was a change in Paul that
I simply could not put my finger on. He was still wooden.
Still monotonous. But at moments of great passion, there
was... oh, a clumsy rawness about him that I found quite
shocking. That was new. Backstage, it seemed the affair was
still going on. Though Uta was more critical of him now.
I knew that something must have happened in Seattle.

SAN FRANCISCO

A neon sign outside the window throws red light on the wall.

JOE *comes in. Looks at the bed. Gets his toilet bag out of his small suitcase and goes into the bathroom.* UTA *comes in.*

UTA. Joe, you in there?

> JOE *comes out of the bathroom brushing his teeth.*

JOE. I can't do this. It's ridiculous. Why don't you and I take this room, and Paul can go in the single?

UTA. Because the single room is a nursery room and the bed's a cot. Even I can't lie flat in it, and Paul would be doubled up like a bobby pin.

JOE. There must be other hotels.

UTA. There are plenty of others, Joe, but Peggy says they're all full of soldiers like this one. Just make the best of it with Paul. Don't fight, don't fidget and don't hog all the blankets like you do with me.

> PAUL *is at the door.*

Come in, honey.

PAUL. What's the problem? That bed's big enough for two.

UTA (*to* JOE). Hear what he says? You can stop complaining.

JOE. I've stopped. I've stopped. I never started. It's just that the last time I shared a bed with a person of the male sex, I was ten years old and so was he.

PAUL. I used to sleep with four or five when I was a kid and I loved every minute of it. It was one of the unsung pleasures of proletarian life. I'm gonna open the window.

JOE. Why?

PAUL. They're singing outside. It breaks my heart. You oughta hear.

He opens a window and they look out.

UTA. It's a beautiful sound.

PAUL *provides a commentary in Edward R. Murrow style:*

PAUL. 'Brave young men are thronging the streets of San Francisco, some returned from the heat of combat, others bound for every point of the Pacific Ocean. Goodnight and good luck.'

UTA. Just look at those two guys. They're so exhausted they can hardly walk.

JOE. They just got off the boat, that's why they're staggering.

He demonstrates a staggering walk.

Get on board, you gotta find your sea-legs. Get on land, you gotta find your land-legs.

UTA. Joe!

JOE. The fleet is in, the hookers will be happy. 'Hi there, soldier! Wanna good time?' 'My name's Maisie!' 'My name's Tina-Belle!''My name's Florrie!'

UTA. Quit messing about. It's bedtime.

PAUL *closes the window.*

JOE. You're right, you're right. Ladies and gentlemen, in deference to the mixed company, I don't propose to strip entirely. Paul, you will oblige me by keeping on your boxers and anything else that might protect my virtue.

He takes off shoes, socks and trousers. Meanwhile:

Which side do you want?

PAUL. I don't know, Joe. Which side do you normally take?

UTA. Joe thinks that sleeping on your left side might cause your heart to stop overnight, so he sleeps on the right of the bed with one arm over his head, like this.

She demonstrates.

PAUL. Jesus Christ, that's complicated. Do what you like, I'm easy.

JOE. I got three pillows here. Who wants two?

PAUL. You do.

JOE. Thank you, Paul. What else can I provide you with? Glass of water? Aspirin? Hot-water bottle?

PAUL. I need the john.

UTA. You can see where it is. Close the door!

   PAUL *goes into the bathroom, closing the door behind him.*
   JOE *gets into bed.* UTA *sits on the side of the bed.*

   Are you gonna sleep okay?

JOE. I'll try. How's your cot?

UTA. It's sweet. There are teddy-bear transfers on the bars. What'd'ya want to do tomorrow?

JOE. You decide.

UTA. Let's go for a ride in a cable car.

JOE. That'd be cool.

UTA. Just you and me.

JOE. That's what I meant.

UTA. After the show, we can eat in Chinatown. Wonton soup, crab rangoon, orange chicken.

JOE. Sure, that'd be nice.

   PAUL *comes back, carrying his shoes and trousers.*

PAUL. Not interrupting, am I?

JOE. We're planning our future. Come right in.

   PAUL *gets into bed.*

UTA. I'll see you guys in the morning. Sleep well.

   She starts to go.

JOE. Hey, Ma! Won't you kiss us goodnight?

PAUL. And read us a story?

JOE. Bring us a mug of cocoa?

PAUL. Sing us a lullaby?

UTA. Goodnight!

JOE. Goodnight.

PAUL. Goodnight.

JOE. Oh, nurse! Will you change my catheter please?

UTA. Just go to sleep!

She goes.

JOE. Do you want the light off?

PAUL. It can stay for a while.

He opens a book, scans a page or two.

You know, you won't be hurting my feelings if you wanna go find Bianca.

JOE. Not tonight. She's sharing with Emilia. It's like the old woman who lived in a shoe down there. Lodovico's in an armchair in the lobby. Cassio's on a sofa in the manager's office. And you know what? I don't mind not seeing Bianca.

PAUL. No?

JOE. There are times when I look at Uta and I ask myself, 'Why the hell do I monkey around?'

PAUL. You struck it lucky with your lady.

JOE. Sure did.

PAUL *reaches out and turns off the bedside light.*

First time I saw her, she was playing Ophelia in a folksy theatre set-up in the countryside. I'd been told about this wacky seventeen-year-old who went running around the fields collecting rue and rosemary for her mad scene. I thought,

'What a pretentious little fool she's gonna be.' Then, when I saw her act, I was so knocked out I couldn't get up the courage to even talk to her. A couple of years later, we got cast in a play in Ridgefield, Connecticut. We fell in love and that was it. She's got a super-über-cultured family, Mahler and Mozart echoing down the hall, bookshelves groaning with Proust and Thomas Mann in French and German and I doubt they really wanted another actor in the family. But they came round to me in the end. I love her, Paul.

PAUL. Any chance we could lose that neon through the window?

JOE. I'll do it.

He goes to the window. Opens it a crack, looks out. Singing is heard more quietly.

The war will be over soon.

PAUL. So they say.

JOE. It's not gonna be the same.

PAUL. I hope it won't. I hope for a better world.

JOE. I mean, it won't be the same for you.

PAUL. Why's that?

JOE. The Russians won't be our loyal allies any longer. You'll need to zip up your lip in that department. No more fulsome words of praise for Uncle Joe Stalin. Hear what I'm saying, pal?

PAUL. I'm not gonna junk what I believe in for the sake of an easy life. I'll speak my mind.

JOE. Suit yourself.

He closes the window, adjusts the blind and gets back into bed. Some red light can still be seen. PAUL gets out of bed and puts his trousers and shoes back on.

What are you doing?

PAUL. I think I'll see if the bar's still open. You'll stay in bed, I suppose?

JOE. I suppose I will.

PAUL *goes to the door.*

Say, Paul.

PAUL *stops and turns.*

PAUL. What?

JOE. You forgot your tie.

PAUL *checks.*

PAUL. Oh, so I did.

He collects it.

Goodnight.

JOE. Goodnight.

PAUL *gives* JOE *a smile and goes.*

UTA

UTA. Paul and I staggered on till the end of the tour, although we never quite recovered from that terrible fight we had. And when Joe and I split up, Paul seemed to find me a lot less interesting and it wasn't too long before we tapered off to zero. My morale was on the floor and I was broke. What saved my life was an offer to take over Blanche in *Streetcar* for the tail-end of New York and a long, long tour.

Paul's political notoriety had come to a head in a redneck town by the name of Peekskill. He was due to sing in aid of Civil Rights but, when he appeared, a riot broke out. There were fist-fights in the streets, car windows smashed, and the audience was attacked with baseball bats while the cops stood by with grins all over their faces. Two days later, in that same park, Paul gave the angriest speech he'd ever made.

I was in my dressing room in Chicago, reading about it when, to my astonishment, Paul walked in. Four years had passed since I had seen him. We planned a drink in the bar of my hotel, but he spotted an FBI man who'd been on his tail all day, he said, so we went up to my room to talk, which was a strange experience. The thrill had gone. The emotional dizzy spell. It was like going back to your childhood home and thinking, 'Is that what it was like? It seems smaller now.' At a pause in the conversation, with a charming air of 'Let's get this over with,' he made a pass at me, which I declined, I thought conclusively. But then...

CHICAGO

UTA *is taking off her make-up with cold cream.* PAUL *opens the door without knocking and looks in.*

PAUL. Hi there!

UTA. I thought you were going.

PAUL. I left my hat.

UTA *looks around and sees it.*

UTA. You've found it.

PAUL. So I have.

UTA. Goodnight.

He takes it.

PAUL. He's out there now.

UTA. Who is?

PAUL. The FBI man. He's pretending to jiggle with a lock.

She looks at him, not believing a word.

See for yourself.

She goes to the door and peers out.

UTA. You're right, he is.

PAUL. Can I stay for a moment till he goes away?

UTA. Just for a moment.

She goes back to taking off her make-up in a business-like fashion.

PAUL. What's this I saw the other day, about some hot-shot theatre director who's taken over your mind like a Svengali?

UTA. He's just helping me to be a better actress.

PAUL. Are you a couple?

UTA. We could be moving in that direction.

PAUL. What is it about you, Uta, that you've always got to be dominated by some overbearing male?

UTA. What?

PAUL. First Joe, who didn't allow you to spend a dime. Then me, who tried to kill you in Seattle, and now this guy persuading you that he's turned you into a wonderful actress when you always were a wonderful actress?

UTA (*dry*). I don't know, Paul. I guess I'm just naturally submissive.

PAUL *laughs*.

What's so funny?

PAUL. You're the bossiest lady I ever met!

UTA. That's an interesting paradox to consider.

PAUL. I won't forget that night in Seattle.

UTA. Me neither.

PAUL. It taught me how to release my anger. I do it all the time now. Changed my life.

UTA. I got something out of it as well.

PAUL. Mind telling me what?

There's a brief silence as he watches her.

UTA. When I was doing this play in New York, there were cast replacements and vacations and at one point, believe it or not, we actually ran out of Stanley Kowalskis.

PAUL. He being the Pole?

UTA. Correct. So they sent for the actor who'd created the role, no less than Marlon Brando.

PAUL *whistles in admiration.*

He arrived after the half with no rehearsal, though he hadn't done the show in over a year and a lot had changed. Different blocking, different rhythms and a very different Blanche in the shape of me. Marlon and I looked at each other thinking, 'This is crazy,' but we heard the audience over the Tannoy, and we couldn't let them down, so on we went, just knocking it backwards and forwards between us and we were... we were pretty damn good.

PAUL. I bet you were.

UTA. Then we got to the scene where Stanley has to rape me.

PAUL. And?

UTA. Whenever I'd done that scene before, it was easy to feel afraid, because the actor was so undisciplined that he would beat me black and blue without meaning to. But looking at Marlon, I saw an actor in complete control. I knew there would be no accidents, no fumbling, nothing clumsy. Simple genius. I thought, 'Where the hell am I gonna find my fear?' Then I remembered you.

PAUL. Uh-huh?

UTA. I remembered your fury. I remembered feeling quite certain that I was gonna get killed. I put you, Paul Robeson, onstage as Stanley and the scene went right like never before. When we came off after the call, Marlon said, 'Did you ever have such a good time onstage in all your life?' He was right. I hadn't. I'm not saying that what you did in Seattle was forgivable, because it was not forgivable, and it never will be. But you gave me something that I could use. And now you really do have to go.

PAUL. Goodnight.

He smiles, peeks out into the corridor, and goes.

UTA waits, giving him time to get out of earshot. Then she moves quickly and decisively to the door and bolts it.

PEGGY

PEGGY. 'Are you now or have you ever been...?' The fateful
question asked of hundreds, thousands of Communists,
ex-Communists and people who'd never had a Communist
thought in all their lives. Entire careers were wrecked,
friendships destroyed. I was born in America when my
mother and father were on tour, and it's been very good to
me, better than England, I may say. It made me sick to see
this spirit of intolerance taking over. I had a personal interest,
that is true. I had a friend, an actress. She'd had cancer and
was slowly getting over it when she was called to testify
before the Committee. It shattered her. She never recovered.
Lost the will. I'd wake up at night to hear her crying, so I'd
put my arms around her, and we'd try to pretend that I was
helping, but I wasn't really. She was Jewish and she'd lived
in Germany during the 1930s and she was afraid that the
same thing would happen all over again.

Takes out her handkerchief, wipes her eyes.

And so she died.

LOS ANGELES

Hotel room. PEGGY *is packing a suitcase.* JOE *is there.*

JOE. When I opened the letter, I thought, 'What the fuck have I done to deserve this? What will they do to me? Am I looking at some hideous…?'

Pause.

Are you gonna go on packing while I talk?

PEGGY. I'm flying back to New York after lunch, so I can't stop now. If you'd come yesterday evening as we agreed, we might have…

JOE. I was all tied up post-synching. There's about fifteen technicians involved. You can't just call the studio and say…

PEGGY. Joe, dear, I know how important you are, so why don't you simply say what you've come to say?

JOE. That's what I'm doing! Jesus!

Pause while PEGGY *goes on packing.*

So, there's my legal adviser next to me, I see a row of stony faces on the podium and the hall is packed. The Chairman says…

PEGGY. Yes, I know how those terrible people work. I thought you were here to explain why you gave in to them.

JOE. Can you not understand…?

PEGGY. I'm trying to…

JOE. …at this moment, as we speak, I am in post-production for a remarkable movie. *Moulin Rouge*, life and art of Toulouse-Lautrec, John Huston directing, brilliant script, incredible leading role for me and the word on the street is it's gonna pick up six or seven Academy Awards, myself hopefully included.

PEGGY. Lucky fellow.

JOE. Yes, well, leaving my vanity out of it, I have a duty *not* to damage the movie's chances by some adolescent gesture of defiance. So when I was told to testify, that's what I did.

PEGGY. It wasn't just testifying, though, was it? It was naming names. It was accusing people of being Communists.

JOE. No, that's a wild exaggeration. I don't even know if Paul is a Party member. What I do know is that his political views are of the *extreme* left, and he never stopped telling me how much he loved the Soviet Union, so by naming Paul as a Commie *sympathiser*, I wasn't doing him any harm.

PEGGY. No, that's not true. The testimony of somebody who was once a close friend carries *enormous* weight. But what I would like to know is why name me? I'm not a Commie. I'm just a boring old do-gooder.

JOE. I said nothing to the contrary...

PEGGY. ...yes, you *did*...

JOE. ...until the final moments when they brought up this telegram of good wishes...

PEGGY. ...to the Moscow Art Theatre...

JOE. ...on its fiftieth anniversary. I signed that telegram, as did you, as did Uta, as did many people that we know. 'Happy Birthday to the Moscow Arts from your American fellow-actors.' And now, three years later, to my chagrin, it gets picked up as evidence that I'm a...

PEGGY. ...'a Russia-loving fellow-traveller'.

JOE. ...so I was shocked and caught off-balance and you know what happened.

PEGGY. I'd still like to hear your version.

JOE. There isn't a 'version', Peggy. They wanted to know who asked me to sign this stupid fucking telegram, and I said it was you. Which is the truth, but...

PEGGY. Had you any idea how…?

JOE. Will you hear me out? Just will you? Jesus Christ.

Pause.

Do you know how scared I was? It was like being onstage except I don't know what the play is, and I don't remember a line, or what my character is, or am I playing myself, and if that's who I'm meant to be, who am I?

PEGGY. Quite existential.

JOE. Plus looking into another broken marriage and disgrace and bankruptcy and ruin.

PEGGY. Well, the effect on me has been disastrous. I was a highly-sought-after director and now I'm practically a pariah. I had a full year planned and that's all gone. Why do you think I'm here in Los Angeles giving my 'Women in Shakespeare' lecture for the umpteenth bloody time? I need the cash. I don't understand it, Joe. Was I disrespectful to you when we did *Othello*?

JOE. No.

PEGGY. Did I sap your confidence…?

JOE. Not at all.

PEGGY.…because for me, the entire experience felt quite blest.

JOE. I loved it too.

PEGGY. It was a joy to see blacks and whites sitting together in the audience. With an actor of colour up on stage. We made that happen. I never doubted that we were doing the right thing. Did you?

JOE. No, never. That was… Yep. It was. It honestly was.

Pause.

I oughta…

A glance at his watch finishes the sentence.

PEGGY. Yes, and I must finish packing.

She hesitates, then makes a decision.

All right, I'll ask. When you named Paul to the Committee, was it revenge for his affair with Uta?

JOE *is taken aback.*

JOE. How do you know about that?

PEGGY. My dear, I've been in the business all my life. Although I kicked myself when I finally worked that one out. *Was* it revenge?

JOE *thinks.*

JOE (*with surprise*). Yes. It was.

PEGGY. Had you been planning it all through the tour?

JOE. No.

PEGGY. What prompted it?

JOE. It was in San Francisco. Paul and I had to share a bed, remember? Uta was on the floor below. Paul got up, to go to the bar, he said. Only he hadn't put his tie back on. You see what I'm saying?

PEGGY. No, I don't.

JOE. Remember how perfectly he always dressed? As though one little hint of sloppiness would dishonour the whole of the black race? There was no way Paul Robeson was gonna appear in a bar without a tie. He wasn't going to the bar. He was going to her.

PEGGY. So you had no idea until then?

JOE. That's not the point. It was the blatancy. He didn't give a fuck whether I knew or not. That was the insult.

PEGGY. Yes, it's those little clues that tell you the most.

She looks round the room.

Now have I everything?

She has.

It is just possible, Joe, that I can scrape a show together. It would be at the City Center, late next year.

JOE. Why are you telling me?

PEGGY. Because my status not being what it *used* to be, I need to offer them a star. Might you be interested?

JOE. I guess I owe you a favour.

PEGGY. I think you do.

JOE. What is the play?

PEGGY. *Richard III.*

JOE. I'll give it serious thought.

He morphs into the role:

Why, I can smile, and murder whiles I smile,
And cry 'Content' to that which grieves my heart,
And wet my cheeks with artificial tears,
And frame my face to all occasions.
Can I do this, and cannot get a crown?
Tut, were it farther off, I'll pluck it down.

HARRISBURG

PAUL *is reading. He wears glasses. There's a knock at the door.*

PAUL. Come in.

It's UTA.

UTA. Hello, Paul.

PAUL. My God, it's you. This is incredible. Wow. Amazing. Come here, honey.

He hugs her and kisses her.

You've not come for the concert, have you?

UTA. Yes, I have.

PAUL. All the way from New York?

UTA. New York to Harrisburg? It's not that far. Besides, I wanted to talk.

PAUL. Anything special?

UTA. It can wait. You look well.

PAUL. I'm fine, I'm fine. Oh, why are we standing here like this? Take a seat. Not that chair, this one's more comfortable. I have nothing to offer you, sad to say. If I'd known you were gonna be here, I would've...

UTA. Don't worry, I brought you a present.

She gives it to him.

PAUL. My, oh my. Can I open it now?

UTA. Of course.

He opens it.

PAUL. Bottle of rum. That's wonderful, Uta. Let me put it some place for after the concert.

UTA. Don't get this wrong, but I might have to shoot off before the end. I need to catch the last train.

PAUL. Of course you do. So why procrastinate?

He rummages round finding some glasses.

I hope you're not gonna miss the best of me. I take longer to warm up these days but, once I've hit the spot, I'm good as ever. Have you bought a ticket? I can slip you one if you need it.

UTA. Don't worry. I can get one at the church.

PAUL. Whatever you want. I've got a warm-up here at six o'clock, but I'll point you in the right direction. It's just a little honest-to-God people's church, like the one my father used to preach in. Yours will be one of the few white faces in the audience. You'll get a warm welcome, I can promise you that.

He gives her a glass of rum and pours a glass for himself but doesn't drink.

UTA. Thank you.

PAUL. I don't know how in the world you found me here.

UTA. I had a tip-off.

PAUL. Did you now? And who was...?

UTA. It doesn't matter who. I walked past this place a couple of times, not realising it was a hotel.

PAUL. It's a hotel of sorts. The little old lady who lives downstairs rents out rooms to friends of the church. It was she let you in when you rang the bell, I suppose?

UTA. I guess it was.

PAUL. She'll fix you a sandwich, if you want one.

UTA. I'm fine.

Each waits for the other to say something, though neither of them does. There's no embarrassment between them. After a while:

PAUL. Are you doing a play right now?

UTA. I'm in rehearsal for *St Joan*.

PAUL. That's a wonderful play. A truthful play. And how is your life now? Where are you living?

UTA. In New York. I held on to the place in Ossining for as long as I could, but eventually I had to sell it.

PAUL. I'm sorry about that.

UTA. It's very sad. I miss it like hell.

PAUL. Do you see anything of Joe?

UTA. We keep in touch about our daughter. He's in Los Angeles a lot of the time these days.

PAUL. I never heard, did he marry Bianca?

UTA. They got married and they divorced. Joe married again, he got divorced again and after that I lose track.

PAUL. Is he still angry?

UTA. With you or with me?

PAUL. Either. Both.

UTA. He feels more let down by you, because he loved you more.

PAUL. But not more than he loved you?

UTA. Oh, absolutely. No doubt about that. And you loved him.

PAUL. I did.

UTA. I loved him too. Then there was you.

PAUL. No, then there was me and you and Joe, all three of us. I hated feeling that I was sharing you.

UTA. You never shared me for a moment. Not really. Not here.

She indicates her heart.

It was you and me. We were a couple. Didn't you know that?

She waits for some acknowledgement of what's she's said.
PAUL *looks thoughtfully at his glass. Then:*

PAUL. I shouldn't be drinking this. I've not been well.

UTA. Uh-huh.

PAUL. It wasn't serious. Just a middle-aged man's complaint.
But they messed up the operation, so I was stuck in that damn
hospital for over a month! Essie was good to me while I was
there. We're sharing a house now, you know. In Harlem.

UTA. Yes, I heard.

PAUL. We get on fine now, Essie and I. We went to Moscow
together five, six years ago. That was the last place I went
before the State Department took my passport off me.

UTA. That must have been…

PAUL. I don't like talking about it.

UTA. It's just that…

PAUL. Enough is enough. Leave it alone.

*From below, a pianist is heard quietly playing the
accompaniment to 'Shenandoah'.*

Hear that? It's my accompanist. The old lady lets him practise
on her piano. He's just a young fellow who lives locally, but
he has a most beautiful touch. It's remarkable how much talent
you can find among the unknown people of the world.

Pause.

We were talking about my passport.

UTA. Not if you…

PAUL. There is no constitutional basis whatsoever for what
they did! I've been pursuing them through the courts. I won't
give up. I have a legal training, don't forget. Just one more
burst is needed and then I will get that passport back. I've
had incredible offers from abroad. Paris, Havana, Moscow,
Tel Aviv and, and other places too. And when I win my case,

a whole bunch of other things are gonna go right for me as well. The concert halls will open up. The touring dates. The radio stations and the record sales. I could even play Othello again, as long as I'm not too old!

He laughs.

That's not a worry for me! I'll be fighting fit. I had a bad spell, but now it's over. Have some more rum.

He goes to get it.

UTA. I heard about that.

PAUL *stops and doesn't pour.*

PAUL. What did you say?

UTA. You said you had a bad spell.

PAUL. Maybe I did. Who told you about it?

UTA. It doesn't matter.

PAUL. It must have been someone. Was it Essie?

UTA. Yes, it was.

PAUL. But how…?

UTA. She called me up.

PAUL. She should never have done that! Never!

UTA. She was worried about you.

PAUL. Now she's got *you* worried too. This is a raid on me by hysterical women!

UTA. It's not like that, you stubborn old mule! We're trying to help!

PAUL. That's how you see it, is it?

He waits for an answer. Slowly subsides.

Yes, I suppose it is. What did she say?

UTA. She said there was a change in you after the operation.

PAUL. You could put it like that.

UTA. Tell me.

PAUL. It was nothing much.

UTA. Like what?

PAUL. Well, to put it simply, I realised how much my life was gonna be limited by this passport business. You know how it is.

UTA. No, I don't.

PAUL. I love America and it's a vast country, but if you can't travel outside it, even that huge vastness becomes a prison.

UTA. Sure.

PAUL. A prison without any bars. But still a prison. That hit me hard. I couldn't...

UTA. What?

PAUL. I couldn't see the point.

UTA. The point of what?

PAUL. The point of any damn thing at all.

UTA. She told me that too.

PAUL. Well, she would know. Best thing, it seemed to me, was keep out of sight for a while, so I stayed in bed.

UTA. How long for?

PAUL. Oh, I don't know. Time passed me by. It bothered me to have any light around me, so I kept the curtains closed. I didn't eat.

UTA. How were you feeling?

PAUL. I wouldn't say you could call it 'feeling'. There was an emptiness inside me, so strong and powerful that it...

UTA. What?

PAUL. ...it seemed to take me over. It seemed like everything I had ever done was worthless.

UTA. But that's not true.

PAUL. It makes no difference whether it's true or not. Strange though it seems. That is a fact.

UTA. How did it end?

PAUL. Just ended.

UTA. No, it didn't.

PAUL. You're right in a way. Essie called a doctor. He said I'm a perfect specimen for my age.

UTA. But what?

PAUL. He thought that I was depressed. His word, not mine.

UTA. And?

PAUL. He gave me some pills. Essie was looking over my shoulder to make sure I took them, so I did. I take them still when I feel inclined.

UTA. Do they help?

PAUL. I don't know. Some days are better than others. Some days are...

He stops. Buries his face in his hands. He cries deeply, powerfully, his whole body shaking.

I don't fucking know.

UTA *goes to him.*

UTA. It's okay.

PAUL. You call this okay?

She waits.

I'm so ashamed at letting you see me like this.

UTA. It's only me.

He disengages from her and moves away.

PAUL. Is that what you came to talk about? My so-called breakdown?

UTA. There's more.

PAUL. Hand me that rum. Then you can tell me.

She brings him the untouched glass and he drinks.

I'm listening.

UTA. You've made a lot of enemies. You always will. But you can handle that. You're better than them. You're stronger than they are.

PAUL. You don't have to flatter me.

UTA. I've not finished.

PAUL. Go on.

UTA. There's just one place where they will always win and where you're always gonna lose. It's Russia.

PAUL. Russia?

UTA. Every time you say that it's the land of the free and the hope of the future and the rest of that shit, you give the people who hate you all the excuse they're looking for to call you a traitor to your country. Though that's the last thing that you...

PAUL. Hold on, hold on. This is a complex issue. Remember the meetings I used to drag you along to? 'The USSR has no Jim Crow, no segregation. But to get a result like that, you've gotta have clear political guidance. Same as...'

UTA. Paul, this is bullshit. It's not about politics. It's not about Russia, even. It's about you throwing away everything you've built up over your whole life. It's self-destruction, Paul, and I hate to see it.

PAUL. What would make you happy? What do you want?

UTA. Stop lying about Russia. Just tell the truth about it. If you won't do it for yourself, do it for me. I know I matter to you. You pretend I don't, but it's all a fake. No one has ever loved you as much as I did. You were my obsession for a year and a half. You were everything to me. You made me cry, you made me laugh, you were my whole fucking existence. I'd

have done whatever you wanted. I'd have married you in
a heartbeat. I would even have given up acting for you,
which is the greatest sacrifice I can imagine. Do what I ask.
Just tell the world what it's like over there. Because you
know. You've been there over and over. It's a terrible
country. It's a tyranny. People are suffering. Say it. Tell
a reporter. Any reporter. It will be the story of the week.

PAUL. What then?

UTA. Your life will change. You'll get some bookings back. It'll
take time, but they can't be fewer than you've got right now.

PAUL. And?

UTA. Some cock-eyed radio station will play a track of yours
and, bit by bit, the others will do the same. The people who
always loved you will feel free to say they love you, and
more people will join them. And you'll get your passport
back, which is *not* gonna happen the way things are.

PAUL. I believe in what the Soviet Union stands for. I rejoice in
its ideals. Maybe too much.

He stops.

UTA. I'm listening.

PAUL. There is a man who comes to mind called Robert
Robinson.

UTA. What about him?

PAUL. He was a factory worker in Detroit. A black man, hired
below the grade that he should have been hired, because of
his race. One day, a team arrived from the Soviet Union,
looking to take on workers for the Five-Year Plan. They
offered good conditions over there and better pay, so he took
the job and he went to Stalingrad.

UTA. What then?

PAUL. He'd hardly arrived when a couple of white Americans
there attacked him, beat him up badly. He was rescued by his
Russian fellow-workers, his attackers were put on trial and, to
his surprise, he discovered one morning that he was famous.

UTA. Because…?

PAUL.…because his story proved that Americans were all racists.

UTA. He was being used for propaganda?

PAUL. Wait. Years went by and, when I was in Moscow, he came to see me in my hotel. We talked a bit, but he was pointing around the room like this…

UTA. It was bugged.

PAUL.…so we went for a walk. He said he'd lost his American citizenship, so he was now just one more Russian guy, like any other.

UTA. Go on.

PAUL. He was living in fear. He knew that even a chance remark could cost him his life. He would arrive at work to find that some fellow-worker had vanished into thin air, and he soon learned not to ask where the man had gone. He was desperate to return back home to America, but the authorities wouldn't let him. He wanted me to ask the high-up politicians I was meeting every day to get him leave to go.

UTA. What did you do?

PAUL. I got Essie to give him my answer.

UTA. Which was what?

PAUL. I couldn't help him.

UTA. Why not?

PAUL. Because I knew that, when he got back home, he would be asked about the Soviet Union, and he might… well, he might say bad things about it.

UTA. You turned him down?

PAUL. I turned him down.

UTA. Where is he now?

PAUL. Still there, I guess. I remember him to this day. The roughness of his workman's hands, the hope in his eyes, his blackness. Don't get me wrong. I *wanted* to help him. I was *longing* to. But then I thought of the pleasure it would give to racists and reactionaries to hear that the lies they'd been spreading about the Soviet Union were not lies after all. That they were true.

UTA. So you betrayed him.

PAUL. I betrayed him for the cause.

UTA. Is that the end of the story?

PAUL. You see, we all possess a treasure in our soul. Something that, if we lose, will leave us damaged for all time. For you, it's acting. If you had given up acting for my sake, you'd be a broken creature now, because acting is what you do and it's what you are. Am I wrong about that?

UTA. It's true.

PAUL. For me, it was my belief that, for all my faults, I'm not a bad man. That, in the balance of my soul, I'm mostly good. That's what I threw away, that day in Moscow. I won't get it back by telling the truth. I can't redeem myself that way. I have to live with the lie.

UTA

UTA. Was that really the reason? Was it the testament of a good
man battered and bruised by what he had done and what had
been done to him? Or just a cover-up for his age-old
stubbornness? As I walked away, I wondered which pocket
of his metaphorical overcoat contained the truth. I wondered
how many truths there were. But at the church that night, he
was himself without reserve, singing with, oh, such warmth,
such heart, such yearning. The pews were filled with quietly
spoken people of colour, respectful at the start and, by the
end, quite overwhelmed. He gave them encore after encore.
It got late. I checked my watch and saw that I'd need to run
to catch the train, so I stood and quietly made my way to the
door. The last I saw of Paul, he was still singing.

INDIANAPOLIS (II)

JOE, PAUL *and* PEGGY *are there.* UTA *stands apart, watching them and remembering.*

JOE. Say, Paul?

PAUL. What, pal?

JOE. Uta and I have got five bucks on whether you sang 'Ol' Man River' at the party tonight.

PEGGY. Yes, what did you do? Tell us.

PAUL. I did and I didn't. You see, I hate to sing about dying and being 'skeered' and getting oh-so weary. It's a hangdog view of life that I can't go along with. So I sing that song in my own home-grown adaptation. It goes…

(With relish.)
'But I keeps laffin'
Instead of cryin'
I must keep fightin'
Until I'm dyin'.
'Cause I will!'

End of play.

A Note About Sources

The play is based on real events. It makes no claim to be an
accurate record of them and much of the action is invented for
dramatic purposes. Certain events are inspired by two
interviews with Uta Hagen, conducted in 1982 and 1984 by the
author of the authorised biography of Paul Robeson, Martin
Duberman. My thanks are due to Professor Duberman and to
the Moorland-Spingarn Research Center at Howard University,
Washington, for making them available to me.

N.W.